MW00774440

The Resurrection
Of The
Meadow

Pendraig Publishing, Sunland, CA 91040
© 2010 Robin Artisson. All rights reserved.
Published 2010
Printed in the United states of America

ISBN: 978-0-9843302-9-4

THE RESURRECTION Of The MEADOW

A Treatise of the Fayerie-Faith &
A Record of Thirteen Occult Formulas & Charms of Art
With Purport & A Sealing Conjuration
& their many useful Sorcerous Permutations
Writ & *Gathered here* on Walpurgis Night AD MMX
For those Inquisitive Adepts who walk
The despised path of *True Sorcery,*
The long-dimmed radiance of the Ancient Gold of the
Wise.

Penned by
Robin Artisson,
Called by some *Ule Heth-Bucca,*
Magister of the *Clandestine Lodge,* called by others the
Covenant of Heth
Hedge-Crosser & Wortcunning Doctor of Fayerie Spirits,
Loyalist of the Undying Court & its Queen

Contained *Herein*

This work is dedicated to *Lady* Annua.

Of The Resurrection of the Meadow

* * *

In times of ancient Elder, ancient Apple-Thorn,
Ancient May & ancient November,
& forgotten ages all wither'd before,
Times of dreaming when *They of Old* walk'd without sin,
& th' tongues of beasts were intelligible to men,
Th' great & cunning seeds were scatter'd
& won purchase in ev'ry hollow to which men gather'd;
For *They of Old* could speak to wood or water
& th' sun & moon traced a living course.
With wood & water & Weird un-split
Tree-mask'd Gods strode among us then;
Fire blazed wi' open mouth of prophecy,
Serpents coil'd round th' gleeful wedding-bed,
& feastful hobbs lurk'd in coals of th' hearth,
They of Old trod th' deep & forest deep again.
Th' fire in th' meadow was a bridge of light
Where Heaven did descend to Earth's delight;
& th' tribute of flesh & tithe in blood
Was wash'd away in th' world's blissful flood.
What but *baleful turning stars* could condemn it so
To hell & fearful plague, th' power then
& th' wisdom inscrib'd in th' healer's art,
& th' notch on th' flying arrow
& th' charm on th' swinging scythe-blade
& th' diviner's clever heart?
Th' *treasure-horde of old* is *more than mere gold*
It is th' art that constrains th' rain to speak again
It is th' art that pries open th' hidden eyes
It is th' art that makes bloom th' rot-dead tree

5

& leaps th' Hedge that never dies.
For we men of late walk th' dying way
& th' world declines to shadow day by day
Th' sepulchral song is all we pray,
& from towers grim declare it a hymn of bliss.
By th' green & ebon Tree of Light
In whose branches th' world is hung a-right,
& th' ghostly hint of forgotten sights-
We must gamble death to emerge quick again.
Dust & bare is th' hope of th' penitent;
& scarce more hope in th' words of sages:
It is shelter of wisdom & brave blood shall win
Th' prize of th' witch'd world, th' mystic,
Th' world reborn, th' feery tree & hill,
Th' *resurrection of th' meadow*, th' death of sin,
& all foulness be consum'd in th' just wrath of ages.
So let ride th' kingly steed of th' Antler-crown'd Lord
King of th' pale men, king of th' slain,
King of th' brown earth where old treasures lay
King of th' fresh furrow, king of th' ancient wood,
King of th' white horn that calls th' feery rade.
Let that *rage-turn'd-hunt* ride forth as before,
To th' *glory of memory* & th' *winning of lore.*

Introduction:
Concerning Purities, Sorcerous Concentration, *And* the Luminous Sense

"Dark was the vaulted room of gramarye
To which the wizard led the gallant knight
Save that before a mirror huge and high
A hallowed taper shed a glimmering light
On mystic implements of magic might;
On cross, and character, and talisman,
And almagest and altar, nothing bright;
For fitful was the luster pale and wan,
As watch-light by the bed of some departing man."

-Lay of the Last Minstrel

Concerning Purity of Body

It is understood that the man or woman who undertakes these rites and charms will do so in a state of *purity,* as well as moving slightly or strongly in the senses of the *Fetch-* using the *Eyes of Fire,* or the *Eyes of Darkness and Luminosity,* alongside the shadowy form or wraith-aspect of every sense. The first degree of the afore-mentioned purity is attained simply by the washing of the face and hands with water from a well, spring or other sacred natural source, which is then mingled with untainted salt; the salt of the sea being the preferable substance.

It is to the "other" aspect or fetch-body of these substances to which one should address their petition of purity. Before the

9

substances are mingled, place the thumbs and forefingers of the hands together forming a triangle, (the triangl'd hand) and hold these two hands over the vessels containing the water and salt, looking and speaking your words of art through the three-sided space of focus. Say unto them: *"Fetch-body of fruitful earth, be mingled now with this fetch of holy water; In the MASTER'S name I call you forth as One; Entity of earth and water, where you are cast, let no contrary power persist or pass."* A hallowed taper is made in a like manner, precisely alike, but with the words *"Fetch-body of living fire, where you pass, let every contrary power retire."*

Make a triple equal-armed cross over the vessel containing both after first circling it thrice with the forefinger of your right hand, thus sealing in the power; the ensorcelled entity of earth and water will maintain its potency for three, six, or nine days beyond the enchantment, growing weaker all the time, and dispersing completely if and when the water is evaporated away or soaked into the ground.

Concerning Purity of Soul and Sorcerous Concentration: The Luminous Sense

Purity of soul is another matter, more recondite. The soul is made pure by *wisdom*, the knowledge of things as they *are* contrary to what men commonly take them to be, or as they *appear*. To see wisely one must see the world using the secret of *sorcerous concentration*- seeing the world as many *and* one simultaneously. Though you look upon many parts and persons every day of your life, you must also deduce and know that your sense of your own differentiated personhood and ego-center must of necessity have arisen from a primal unity to which it could stand in contrast.

10

If we believe the common report of the illumined that this sense of separation may be overcome, then the primal unity must persist, and stir beneath the level of ego-consciousness, for a "new" state cannot be created from something which does not exist; a "new" state or condition is always the re-emergence or re-discovery of something, some precedent or force which is latent, original or ancient.

The Charms contained within this brief work of the Art cannot be done by merely gathering substances and speaking words. The words of force attendant on each of these charms must be spoken from within a consciousness of the *Luminosity*- the Great Sorcerous Light that reveals itself as the "true insides" of everything, the depth of things. It requires the Feery-Trance or the act of Sorcerous Concentration to attain this. For this work I shall set down two methods of attaining to this experience, to bolster the working potential of this book. The first method is called "The Roots of Self as the Roots of a Darksome Tree" and the second is called "Weaving and Dissolving into the World".

To perform the first work, Sit still in some quiet location until you can feel your breath-cycle in your body, and feel your heart beating. Feel the warmth in your skin and the rumble and rush beneath your flesh, the constant involuntary processes of the body always moving forth, whether or not you consciously think of them. For so many of the half-wise, the fact of *involuntary activity* in and of the body is a sign of a foreign power working its will upon them; by virtue of the fact that we do not "control" the heart beat, the fact that "we" do not beat our own hearts, we view it as a relatively foreign process. Certainly we depend on the involuntary beat of the heart, but we view it as a process happening *to* us, not a process *of* us.

11

Feel your heart and breath. You will notice that when one brings attention to the breath, it suddenly changes in rhythm- suddenly, your attention, which found it involuntarily breathing away, shocks it into conscious control, and it requires a bit of forgetting to let it go back to breathing without your will to set its pace. Unlike the heart, the reins of the breath can be taken by the conscious will and altered. But for this technique, we do not wish to alter it; like the heart, we wish to just feel it and let it do whatever Fate has it doing at the moment.

Now, understand that all over your flesh and body, countless involuntary processes are taking place- you are a great cosmos of activity and power and transformation. And your entire conscious awareness has no clue of the immensity of the body's workings- this very fact, true of the human body, would seem to reflect how we humans seem to look upon the universe as a whole- tiny minds, gazing upon an immense cosmos with countless processes and laws and events that we have no conscious knowledge of, no way of estimating or conceiving of.

Man's sense of isolation begins in his own body when he refuses to define as "himself" anything he doesn't understand or control. The narrow range of consciousness that you experience your body with defines as "itself" as only those things it can *control*- your memories (though they can hardly be described as perfectly "controlled") your thoughts, your imaginations, your goals, your ideas, your opinions. If one looks closer, even all those things that we identify as "ours" easily are unstable and would seem to have a mind of their own very often, or rush out of our control, but we shall leave that fact be for now. Let me only say that this single fact of the illusion of control, if meditated upon, could yield immense wisdom.

12

Our sense of isolation is linked to how we cannot get to the *roots* of our own beings and see that what we really and truly "are" isn't encapsulated by our conscious range of identity. We do not normally identify the beat of our own hearts, our most essential bodily process, with either "ourselves" or our "control", but in reality, the deepest core of our being *is* beating our own heart.

At the roots of you as an entity, is a power that is willing all of your bodily processes to occur- even those you call "involuntary". You are living; you are beating a heart; you are breathing a body; you are willing fire in the blood and belly to metabolize food; all of it is *you expressing yourself*, from the deepest roots. You do not normally experience it that way at all, but you can by reverting to your being-roots.

It is those roots that we desire to reach, for in those roots, at that deeper seat of the human, is another perspective on reality which allows one to see with another sort of seeing. And it is a profoundly simple matter: when you fix upon your breathing and heart beating, simply let your awareness regress to the "area within" which is "below" your lungs and heart, "below and behind." You let your awareness regress by gently willing it so, and letting yourself feel as though your awareness is drifting downward and deeper like a snowflake on strong, soft wind.

"Below and behind" your heart and lungs would, literally speaking, be your back, and the world behind your back, but that isn't where your awareness must go; the metaphysical "below and behind" of this technique is a dark place, a dark root-bog from which the tree of your body and brain is growing, an unseen, deep place which only the imaginal

13

function of the mind might be able to give a form to. But you need no vision; you need only a feeling of it.

Engage the poet in you, and "go to the roots of your being". You can picture it as your deepest, darkest insides if you like; the awareness-shift certainly always seems to be "lower", but the work is simple and truly effortless if you just let it happen. Go to the roots of your being, until you can sense that something deep and dark is making your heart beat, and your breath happen- and know that this "something deep and dark" is not separate from you; it is *more* of you, a *deeper* you, outside of your typical consciousness. The focus on the heart and breath will always remind you and assure you that it is there, for their operation is evidence of its dark and hidden will.

Open up your identity; accept that there is more to you than you normally see or sense, and let yourself become the power that is beating your heart as another method of self-expression, the power that is breathing and metabolizing as another means self-expression. You typically express yourself in words; this deeper part of you *self-expresses* in terms of bodies and organs and systems and the like.

Once you have succeeded, your world will change with power. From your own roots, you can now sense- directly and indirectly sense, using the intuition and the mind- the "roots" of other beings. Other humans, trees, animals, even the great Earth and Sky: just like you, they have a deeper being, which is *expressing itself* as the things your eyes see. Earth and Sky are easiest; when you have gone to your roots, the root-powers of Earth and Sky are immense and everywhere apparent; they are the easiest to feel and intuit. You are "seeing" and sensing

14

with your luminous senses now, and the luminosity of other things is what you are sensing.

Earth and Sky's great depth is our true parent-origin; the depth of you is the same as the depths of them. All things in this world grew from the depths; not from the hands of a clay-shaping or vase-making creator were things "made"; *things timelessly emerged and grew from the deep.* See your world this way, and find peace in it. At death, a full reversion to the deep is at hand.

This depth-state is easy to achieve and maintain, with practice- but never too much effort. You can walk around in this condition, feel the deep darkness in you and in all things, the great luminous voids of mystery that all things seem to be emanating from by various acts of will. And when you master this, one step remains- to *speak* from it.

The Art of incantation, invocation, or word-conjury is the art of speaking from the roots of yourself directly to the roots of another entity or thing. Your spoken words are only the "middle" of the process- the process begins deep in you, in your roots, comes up from you into words, goes to the intended subject, and descends to their roots. With further mastery, one will uncover the capacity to *"speak from darkness to darkness"*, using no outward words, but still projecting power or willing communication from ones own roots into the roots of another being or reality: an invisible, silent "voiceless voice."

It is this silent voice that I have used for years to summon my Puckril-Fetch so many times- but the truth is always this: if you *can* use spoken words, do it, for they add a strong level of power to any art, another layer of expression, especially for works of the Art that intend to manifest coarse, non-subtle changes in the outward world. But for inward communication, speaking from the roots is the key and secret, for your root, like the root of all things, is the *Unseen World*, the unifying home of all spirits and powers, the origin-world of all things that come to be seen, and all things that remain unseen.

Now, with this knowledge thus given, you can truly use the incantation given before for the purification Charm of Salt and Water. If at any time during this working you should find that stray and intrusive thoughts and images of the imagination disrupt your focus, do not try to will them away; the tension created by the effort- the "energy of resistance"- only maintains the distraction. Instead, use the thoughts and images as objects to help bolster your regression to the roots: the fact that thoughts and images should arise from you proves again that the hidden depths of you have "sent out" some manifestation of self. "Follow the thought" back to the roots; "follow the image" back to the depths from which it came, and you will defeat all obstacles in this way.

The other method of achieving the Luminous Sense is "Weaving and Dissolving Into The World"- if one cannot go "inward", one can go "outward" and find the same depth. Take a stone of some type, or a small handful or earth, and a few leaves from various shrubs and trees, and have some water at hand- or better, go out of doors to be exposed to all the forms of natural substance, and, upon relaxing, gently will your mind to fix upon the kinship between flesh and dark soil and humus, between wind and breath, between blood and water, and thus enter the "great weaving" which is reality of your oneness with elemental things, all things, everywhere. Recognizing how the "stuff" of your body and soul is the stuff of the world is an easy way to "break out" and enter into the greater reality.

16

Of course, you aren't "entering", ultimately, some great, new state; you are rediscovering an ancient and timeless way of being that you always had. We forget, due to our narrow focus, that our relationship and connection to the world is something we *have*, and we begin to fixate on the idea that it is a thing we must *form* or *create*. But it is only that fact that we already have it in the first place, intimately so, that allows us to seemingly "create" it or find it.

Upon doing so, feeling the expansion into the vastness of the inter-connected mass of life and elemental substance, you should have no trouble realizing that within all things- including you- is a great dark space of openness. It is that same dark space that one finds using the technique of the roots. A great union can come about from either the inner trek or the outer dissolution, for they both begin and end in the same place.

In the great union, some transformed sense of the discreet self remains, but now it is seen as not "centered" in an isolated corpse or body- indeed, it never truly was- but instead *arisen* as a spontaneous quality of the interaction of all things in the world or the wholeness. This is the greatest and most powerful insight that the Old sorcerous path can bestow on anyone. In this, any feat of mind or body is possible. A life and death of peace is possible; a true ethic and morality based on organic inter-relatedness is possible.

It is a *pure will* that can bring about the easy transition into the Luminous sense at any time- and what is a pure will? It is a will that is not turned onto vain things, fixed on useless distractions from the true *path* and *meaning* of our lives as human beings. Our lives are here; these bodies exist as extensions of something deathless, powerful, and sacred.

We are vehicles of a greater attainment, which is seemingly beyond this world and simultaneously the most perfect and natural part of it.

We rightly ought to be pious to the Old Ways of experiencing the sacred, giving due and right offerings and honor to the great Otherness and the ruling powers of the Unseen worlds. To offer up our allegiance to them, to place ourselves wisely in their favor and hands- these things purify the will. The practices of the sacred occult paths purify the will, else they are useless.

When you have mastered the sorcerous concentration that allows one to experience the luminous force in body, world, ground, and sky, you will know it easily- you will be able to walk about your daily comings and goings in this state, without its interruption. It will become effortless.

CHARMS *and* FORMULAE

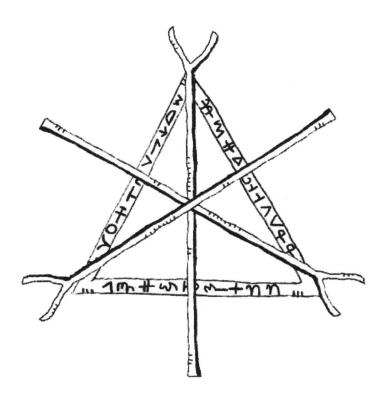

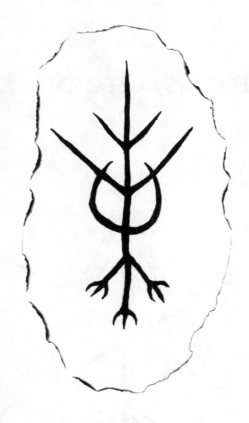

The Faery Tree

Th' *twisting vines* of my words will choke
Th' false prophets to *doom.*
& they *will* know
That these Seeds of th' *Undergreen,*
Born of th' *red* sun & *dead* moon,
Shap'd themselves
By *contort'd* adaptations of Fate
Into rows of *teeth* for my *hungry* mouth.
Th' *Tiddy Mun* reigned a king in th' fens;
Th' *pestilence weird* born in th' bog was his
To command.
Just so, *White* & *Terrible* Queen,
Let th' weird of th' Sour & Sick *serve* me,
As *I* plow & plant th' seeds of your *sacred tree*
& aid it to thrive *again.*
Let *none* approach th' throne of Truth
Without *purging* from their wasted belly
Th' *falsehood* that masquerades
As righteousness
& troubles th' *Land* & *Sky.*

I. Petitioning the Verbena Weird

VERBENA,
Protector of the home, *Bestower* of ev'ry peace in the home,
Healer of dis-ease, *Scatterer* of evil spirits and powers,
Attractor of love, *Preserver* from nightmares

Holy'st wort, Herb of every Grace
Wort of th' Cross, *Joy* of th' Simpler,
Great boon of th' Sorcerous Race:
Vervain Weird, entity nam'd *Verbena*
From th' Garden of th' Green Virgin,
Th' *First of Holy Grounds* you grew;
Entwin'd in th' chaplet of th' Virid Ruler
& the Queen whom *first* you knew,
To travel th' world of *storm* & *fear*
Through ages *vast* & without name
Till you found your seed a purchase *here.*
Now, I come before you, ancient Weird
To petition your *aid,* your *favor* & *grace*
To take of your slender body what I *require.*
Give thy *consent* for my harvest,
This taking done in careful *purity.*
Verbena, be *pleased* to preserve in you
Th' *Weird powe*r for which I yearn.
Not forever will I wander th' earth
With feet of *flesh,* of *water* & *blood*;
When my *life-power* runs into th' *ground*
Take your rightful portion in return.

This precious coin, this honey,
This milk, this blood *into your* earth
This gift from my hand & heart to pay th' *Weird*
To seal our pact *now done.*
Verbena, all th' wise celebrate your worth.

23

PURPORT

The Petition to the Verbena Weird" is a hymn of praise to the divinity of the weird or spirit of the Vervain herb. Such hymns, "words" spoken from the roots of a person to the roots of the other and bound together with voiced words, are not mere poetry or lip-service to a natural sense of fairness between man and nature. Such *words of Art* assure the integrity of the transfer of power between the two agents: the part of the herb sought by the Cunning Man or Woman from the wort is its gift of power; the words and gifts given in return are the balancing factors that maintain *natural justice* and *preservation of force*.

The Verbena weird's body is sought for its gifts; if you are taking only a portion, which will not destroy the plant, a coin, honey, milk, or blood can be placed in a shallow hole near the roots of the plant, using the final portion of the Petition while in the act of giving. If the plant must be destroyed, taken up by its roots, that final portion should be omitted, ending only the "Rightful Portion" pact. The business of ending the outward life-expression entire of a plant, or any entity, is never a thing of little or no moral concern. Plants- the virid bodies of Weirds, reflections of spirit-bodies that maintain a deep and ancient inner life- are not an exception. From the "Garden of the Green Virgin"- Earth in her virginal state, before human beings ravished her with agriculture and industry- came the ancestors of all the worts that we know, as well as our own ancestors.

Herbs still transmit the numinosity of that powerful place, the archetypal untamed and untouched land teeming with spirits and power. It is a place that now lives only in the inner-world, the shining green Meadow that can sometimes emerge into

24

this world at mystical and powerful times. Every plant still carries a memory of that garden, and the blessing of the Green Virgin- the Earth-Entity and All-Mother that first allotted the powers of herbs and simples, and saw, in her darkly intuitive manner, that each of them sprang forth from the depths in a form suited to carry and mediate these powers. All life, including herbs, are protected also by the Virid King- the Lord of Life and Death, whose ancient presence still spies the world through the innocent eyes of the laughing and greenery-vomiting "Green Men" that still hang here and there. Make no mistake; he is the Cthonic mask of the Lord of Earth and Sky- the Faery King, first husband to the Green Virgin.

If you can, draw a circle around yourself and the plant you wish to petition and harvest from with a hazel rod or wand. Take gently what you desire, once the request is made; harvest at the time necessary to your gathering, and better it be with the proper alignment of time, day, and stars, proper to the plant's governing currents and spirits. But before and after all of these considerations, it is *respect* for the holy presence of any wort or plant that makes this sorcery potent. Always wrap harvested wort in a clean white cloth of linen, cotton, or wool- and take it away to proper preparation and storage quickly.

II. A Charm *That Shall Protect* the Meadow

Collect soil, leaves and seeds from the meadow or field
and place them in an earthenware jar or glass bottle full of
honey, along with a pinch of blessed salt, and three small,
consecrated equal-armed crosses of oak tied with red thread.
Seal this vessel well with wax, and bury it in the place that
shall be protected. If only one such jar will be consigned
to the ground, let it be at the center of the meadow. If two,
let one be at the center of the southern half, and one at
the center of the northern half; if three, let it be the same
manner as two with one between them; if four, one at the
center of each quarter of the ground, north, south, east, and
west. When all of the consignments of vessels in the earth
are done, walk about the meadow thrusting hazel or oak
stakes, small and slender, each into the earth, dipped in
milk and honey before they are thrust down. Make a great
square or circular boundary-line of stakes around the entire
meadow, a line of wooden sentries unseen in the ground
always containing within their bounds the burial-sites of the
jars. Then move to the center of the meadow: the charm is
made standing bare of foot upon the earth of that place, and
striking the ground first in each direction thrice with a hazel
staff or wand.

* * *

On th' head of th' *meadow of peace*,
Where bird-wing drifts & green leaves sift
An enchantment of mighty Providence
Is laid within th' roots *most deep*:
People of Twilight who *Watch* & *Ward*
Forbid here harmful turn *of* chance

27

& forbid every *hateful* circumstance.
Let no evil prodigies stray near
Nor th' spectre fear,
Nor let blood be here shed unjust;
Keep *watchful* guard with unseen eyes
'Till your ground *be* split
& th' fires below arise.
& upon *he* who violates this *decree*
Knowing *or* unknowing *though he be*:

HOOIMLEIAN
ARAOOAN
HUAT
HUAT
HUAT

NONA
Let terrors descend on *him*,
DECIMA
'Till he breathes *no* longer.
MORTA

* * *

PURPORT

Honey is a great preserver; the honey in the buried vessels preserves the leaves, simples, and seeds of the meadow in its golden sweetness for as long as the vessels remain unbroken. *By preserving the part, one preserves the whole-* and honey is the sweet golden dew of heaven, of the pollens of the air captured by bees and worked, in the six-sided Hex-power of the hive and comb, into nectar. Honey is a product of a powerful natural sorcery, and has a multitude of functions beyond this ritual creation of sanctified and protected ground. The passage within the incantation which says "is laid within the roots most deep" is being more than just poetic; it is referring to the fact of sorcerous concentration- of the sorcerer or witch speaking from the *roots of the person* to the *roots of the meadow-* a state that must be attained for this work to have power. The "People of Twilight who Watch and Ward" are the spirit-bodies of the pale people, the people of Faerie, merged with the ground in that place, and with the roots of the trees and plants of that place. Both the spirits of the faerie-dead and the powers that dwell in the land there can be present; there is always a large overlap between these two degrees of spirit in folklore.

The "Watch and Ward" refers to those spirits who, for whatever secret reason, are charged with overseeing the transfer of power and the harmony of a particular place. Not all places will naturally have a Watch and Ward- but most tranquil places of any degree of hidden-ness or beauty will. The buried bottle is no offering to them; it is a preservation charm. The milk and honey on the stakes of hazel or oak are their offering- and the boundary made by the wooden stakes is tied to the buried vessels by the honey. The same honey in the jar should be used on the boundary stakes. The death-curse that follows the request for the protection of the meadow or outdoors place is bound to the names HWIMLEIAN, spelled in a half-phonetic form in the charm, and ARAWEN, again spelled half phonetically. They are the great King and Queen of Elfhame, the Pale White Wanderer whose voice utters occult wisdom into the sorcerer's mind in the wilderness, and her consort, the antlered king of the terrible Wild Hunt- the Landwarder, protector of Nature's balance. NONA, DECIMA, and MORTA are the Feery-ladies who rule over Fate, themselves expressions of unfathomable being and necessity.

III. A Feery Feast
(*Hawthorn stream*)

The *feery supper* is best attended to on the high and holy
days of the ancient calendar, or when the moon is full, but
it can be held whenever the need is great or respectfully
required. Retire to a suitable place (ideally) in the twilight
or night when the moon is high, such as the roots of a great
faerie tree, an ancient well, the side of a hidden rural spring,
or an isolated graveyard or ancient burial mound, and make
upon the ground a triangle of white or yellow flour. At the
bottom points of that triangle have two candles blazing; at the
top point, a thurible or suitable vessel with coals to receive
dried vervain, rosemary, and cinquefoil. In the center of that
triangle set a wooden, silver, or earthenware cup and bowl
filled with wine or milk and dark bread, and around the
triangle, if the season be agreeable, fragrant flowers, petals,
and blossoms of the area. If one can manage it, one should
never fail to have hawthorn blossoms or twigs present.
Before the triangle of flour is made, take a bottle of spring
water or some untainted water, and pour a small trickle from
north to south before you, in the name of the Holy Twins
(they who are The Seen and The Unseen, respectively)
bidding the *"trickle-road made here well"* to be a *"ghost road
from beyond the hedge, from the invisible spaces of heaven or
hell."* In a like manner pour a road from the northwest to the
southeast for the Spirit-Host, and another from the northeast
to the southwest for the Good Folk. In this manner, you
form a Hex-sign, three lengths of watery pouring or "spirit
lines" that all meet at a common center, forming a hex. The
center of that hex will be enveloped by the triangle of pale
flour which is drawn afterwards, and the cup and bowl sit on
the perfect center. Trace a circle in the ground around

33

you with a hazel rod and strike the ground around the area thrice to each direction with that same rod once you have completed these formative tasks, then plant the rod in the earth north of the triangle. To the south of the triangle, again cast in flour, or created from twigs, leaves, and pebbles, the sigil of the Faery Tree (emblazoned on one of the pages within this book) should be made. If you are doing this rite indoors at your home, do it before your hearth or stove, and upon a bare floor or table. The room- and home generally- should be swept clean, and straightened away such that you would not be ashamed to have even the most respected person or dignitary visiting. On the hearth or stove-side should be placed a bowl of clean water for the Faerie-people to wash themselves, and a separate bowl of bread and milk for their comfort. Of course one will have washed with the ensorcelled water before beginning.

* * *

Preparatory Invocation

I have *placed* my home in order
I have washed with *hallow'd* water
A circle drawn *perfect* round
& a fire at th' center ground
HWIMLEIAN / HWIMLEIAN / HWIMLEIAN

Exhortation

To th' *Shimmering Gate* in th' Feery Hill
I send *forth* my words of *praise* & *Art*
To th' messenger of th' Queen & King
To th' guardians of hill & stone
To th' *ears* of dead men & women gather'd *together*
& those who wander *alone*:
34

My words are *emblazon'd* on a parchment of *spirit*
I intend them for th' Royal Court of th' Feery people
Its *rulers* & courtiers & Noble Gentry
Descend, my words, to those regions of *darkness* & *awe*
Where lurk th' *treasures* of mortal hopes.

Carry these words away, *loyal messenger,*
Take them to th' thrones of th' Shining Ones
Take them to th' Halls & Feasting Tables *below*
Let them *resound* throughout th' *Unseen.*

Consecration
(spoken through th' triangl'd hand)

Feery King with your *antlered crown*
& your huntsmen & your hounds
Ancient rider of *wood* & *track* called in truth ARAWEN
Behold cup & bread offered in *your* honor
If it pleases *thee*, let your potency come upon *them.*

Feery Queen with your *milk-white* steed
& your sisters & your serving men
Ancient Queen of *peerless beauty* called in truth NINEVE
Behold cup & bread offered in your *honor*
If it pleases *thee*, let your potency come upon *them.*

Benedictions

I lift this cup & give a benediction *fourfold*
Blessings be upon th' People of Peace

Truth & rest on th' *Ancestral dead*
Homage to th' Queen & King of Feery-Elfhame
Honor to th' over-arching darkness of th' Great Unseen

I lift this bowl & I make a *pledge to th' Powers*
Truth, great vessel of peace
Wisdom, second to none
Life, th' light of *sky* & *land*
& th' Cunning of th' hidden Art

Consummation

Here a *portion* of the bread and drink are consumed
by those attending to the rite.

Giving

The remains of the meal are poured onto the roots of a
sacred tree, cast into feery-waters, left at the foot of sacred
stone, or given to the Earth itself. If the Feery-meal was done
indoors, the giving is taken out of doors to a suitable place,
before the incantation is said:

To th' Hollow Hill & th' *Dominion of Feery* this is given
To th' people of th' Dusk World this is given
Down deep & deep again into th' earth
& unto th' regions of *hidden light*
To th' tongues of th' thirsty dead
Th' friendship of th' *pale people*
& th' honor of th' Secret Rulers
Feery-blessings be upon us
& upon th' people in th' deep *below.*

36

PURPORT

This is the Faerie-feast or Red Meal *par excellence-* the rite from which all other meals shared with the Unseen world are derived. Upon this form rests the entire core of the ancient faery-faith, and the potential for bonding the bodies and souls of living men and women with the great powers in the Otherness. This is more than just a religious expression of hope in the unseen; it is a technology for creating enlinkages between the ferth and fetch, between the mortal and the immortal, thus bridging the two worlds until a final union is attained. The meal is itself the "interaction point" between something seen and something unseen and mysterious, yet potent. It is also a kindness to the faery-people, an act of authentic worship, which symbolizes, declares, and shows the truth of union and reciprocal giving between all worlds and all beings. It is the survival of ancient sacrifices and shared meals between Heathen people and the Gods and spirits they adored. The Faery Tree sigil used in this rite- *The Sigil of the Horned Moon Tree-* is a potent ancient symbol of totality, of fierce, implacable fate and the totality of all life, blessings, worlds, and hidden things.

Without this rite, no possibility exists of formal "faery favor"- the blessed state in which a man or woman and their families and possibly communities are blessed and admired by the unseen powers- the end result of which is joy in the soul and serenity in this world. With this favor comes a blessing of peace, prosperity and plenty, as well. Even though the meal itself is a supreme, subtle act of sorcerous might, a further sorcery can be woven into it, after the giving, asking the Faery-people (once one has been favored by them through regular repetition of this rite over some seasons) for favors- by saying or petitioning "In return for these gifts well-given, People of Peace," and adding respectfully what you desire, what you quest for, or what work you need their assistance with.

Of course, this exchange, if they answer with aid, will require a token of gratitude on your part, one that you should not fail to give. This working can be used to give more specific gifts of gratitude to some wight, weird, or spirit- in the *Giving* incantation, simply add the intended's name, and remove some of the others, to make it shorter and simpler. For instance, the standard giving states "to the tongues of the thirsty dead, the friendship of the pale people, and the honor of the secret rulers"- but if you were thanking the Verbena weird for harvesting from its body, you could replace those three lines with "to the honor and increase of the Verbena weird", and then end with the standard two lines as given.

IV. Feast *for the* Convocation of the Meadow

The *Bull*-Feast April 21
The *Virgin*-Feast August 21
The *Goat*-Feast December 21

Gather nine stones of hand-size and select a suitable place at a forest edge, in a hidden forest clearing, in a lonely stand or copse of trees, a meadow or field, or alongside a country lane, or any place where the collectivity of spirits of the land- *the convocation of the meadow*- seem to be powerful, a place where the broad land can be gazed upon easily, but where the Cairn to be made with the stones will not be disturbed. Upon that place, at twilight, make the three Trickle Roads as in the Feery Feast, and draw a triangle of pale flour on top of the watery Hex-sign thus formed. At the center of that triangle, make a small mound of flour, and on top of the flour-mound and triangle, pile the nine stones. Pile them so that you can place a bowl or cup on top. In that vessel, have a mixture of milk, flour, and honey, proportioned and stirred so that it is thin and flowing. You may place a taper at the foot of the cairn, or build a small fire there if it is safe, but this is not fully necessary, though it is powerful.

Trace a wide circle around the Cairn with a hazel rod, and strike the earth three times in each direction before you make the incantation, starting to the south, and turning to face the powers all around:

* * *

Hearken, hallow'd Convocation of th' Meadow

Ye of lonely road, of *woody copse* & bramble
All scatter'd invisibles of th' Weird
That tread th' open grasses & th' tangle

Wards of plow-blade & *ye* who walk th' furrow
Unseen 'mid thieving hare & rasping crow
Protecting th' acres where kine all low-

Hearken Ye in Earth's name, Hearken, Hearken!

In th' name of He of th' Plow'd Field, He of th' Feery hunt,
Rise to sup forthwith from this *brimming* cup
Take ye th' *milk, honey,* & *crumbled flour*
From this pil'd stone, meal & *water.*

Be gleeful strong & comely sooth'd
& fly renew'd to thy tasks at hand
From th' land so fair let grist appear
& forbid *harm* & *mischance* here.

* * *

PURPORT

This service to the Convocation of the Land-Powers creates a sacred space of interaction with them- marked by a sacred Cairn. Every time this feast is done, (and it should be done three times a year, at minimum- the Bull, Virgin, and Goat Feasts, on the days given above) an extra stone is added to the Cairn. Only add a stone on one of the feasts mentioned above; every petition or thankful offering made to the Cairn need not add another stone. Do not add a stone on the first feast; leave only nine. The Cairn must not be molested; if the human guardian or guardians of the Cairn must forever depart the land or somehow lose connection to it, such that strangers may find and disperse the Cairn (a disastrous act that would anger the powers that become used to eating and enjoying themselves there), a pit should be dug to the west of the Cairn and the stones placed respectfully in it, before filling the pit with a good quantity of milk and covering it over.

The offering cup left on top of the Cairn at each feast should, after a few hours or the next day, be poured into the cracks between the stones- and thus it is that all offerings to the Cairn should be given. If favors are sought from the Land-powers, one may, after establishing the Cairn, write a need upon parchment or inscribe a sigil expressing the need, and roll it up, and at twilight, thrust it into the cairn, along with an offering of milk poured over the stones. If the needed aid comes, more milk and bread should be poured and crumbled into the stones. Three stones will be added to the Cairn a year; within the space of just over 30 years, should the Cairn-working go unbroken, 108 stones will be present. After this point, no more stones need be placed, though the feast must go on, three times a year. A Cairn of 108 stones gives birth

41

to a great and masterful Land-wight, a powerful *Weird of the Cairn*, whose connection with the earth, the spirits of the area, and the family or person who is steward to the Cairn surpasses measure. The entire Genius Loci of the area- a collective of all lesser Genii- will coalesce to such a powerful focus.

If your Cairn is for the honor of land-wights of a forest or wood, and there are no plowed fields nearby, then omit the three lines that begin with "Wards of plow-blade and ye who walk the furrow..." and omit the title "He of the plowed field" from later in the incantation, leaving only "He of the Feery Hunt." If the Cairn is for farms, fields, meadows, or any other such place, even with only a few trees nearby, use the entire incantation.

V. Obtaining *by Art* the Hazel Wand

Approach the roots of a Hazel tree at twilight, bringing with you mingled milk, wine, and honey. Pour it in a clockwise circle around the tree, before saying the charm:

* * *

Hazel weird profound, *enhazel'ng* th' sacred ground,
Ev'ry wight smiles to see you grow
No wood was e'er so wise, nor adored *Seeing* so;
Thy green *woody* branch shall smite th' serpent well
Turning back *unwisdom*, th' tangling thorn of hell,
Th' regent soul of Earth finds purity in you.
A *grateful heart* chain'd to *magistry* salutes you here
Weird of th' diviner's *sceptre*, endow me wisely too.

* * *

Take the branch that you need swiftly, with a clean, sharp instrument, and never let it touch the ground at harvesting-capture it in a white cloth of linen, cotton, or wool and carry it away for your use. As you are cutting, ask the weird to *"preserve in this thy branch thy weird and sorcerous might."*

PURPORT

Just as the charm for the Verbena weird discussed and laid down a criteria for the respectful taking of herbs and worts, this charm and its generous offering of mingled milk, wine, and honey to a tree-weird lays down a criteria for taking from trees.

VI. Attaining *to the* Fetch-Self by Binding

Take the letters of your full name and remove any
redundant letters. From the "key letters" left, make a
pleasing sigil. Then, draw a sigil which is precisely reversed
from that one; draw them both on a strip of parchment, the
first at the top, and the reversed under it, like a reflection in
a pond. Put a dab of blood or spittle at the center of both
sigils. When the moon is well "horned", in an early waxing
or late waning, preferably the wane, place the parchment in a
triangle of flour, which the thin hex-lines of water have been
made beneath (taking care never to wet the parchment), and
place a black cloth over the reversed sigil. Place a burning
taper on the "right" sigil, and set to burning dried cinquefoil
and mugwort. A Saturnian wort can be added to the burning
mixture to increase the power of the rite ten fold. When
the work begins, tear the black cloth in two; place the torn
strips to the right and left of the triangle. The best place to
perform this rite, under that moon, is on the edge of a forest
or hedge.

* * *

With a hand of will thrust *forth*
I dismiss th' veil of th' shroud
Across that *thornful hedge* I reach
To th' mask & cloak of th' Fetch.

To tread th' dust & straw of th' land
With th' foot of man is but half my fate;
Th' great *Other* with power I will take
To shift unto th' witch'd self, & mighty,
Under th' horned moon & by forest edge.

45

I am *he* who flies with spirit body & shadow
Encircled by familiars scritching in delight-
This is th' fetch-way of day turned to *night*
Day to *dark*, light to *unlight*, glare to *unbright*,
   An ember passes from sight to unsight
   & lights th' way with *darkling glimmer*
Th' seed of my knowing forever clear:

It is will that drapes me with th' cloak of Fetch
   It is will th' *witch'd mind* hath set
   To th' task of flitting 'mid shadows dim
   Fearless among th' ghast & grim
For I, Man & Cunning, am *feared* among them.
   Th' shroud is torn; th' fetch is bound!
   It comes from beyond th' *bog of night*
   & up from th' deeps of th' *ground*.

* * *

PURPORT

When you speak the words "Day to dark, light to unlight, glare to unbright", blow out the candle on the top sigil, and then move it, smoldering and with the wick still glowing, to the reversed sigil. Do this as you say "An ember passes from sight to unsight." When you say "The shroud is torn, the fetch is bound", move the candle and fold the parchment strip in half, joining the two sigils, and then, roll it up, and use the two black strips of cloth to tie it tight together. That is the talisman this working makes; take that talisman and carry it on your person, and have it upon you when you attempt to enter a trance to reach the Fetch. Always make this attempt immediately after this powerful rite, or, if you are using sleep, hang it around your neck or place it under your pillow to gain the dream-meeting. Try to go to sleep as soon as you can after the working. The next day, the parchment must be untied and burned, whether or not the work succeeded.

The Fetch has two meanings here, either of which can be used for the object of the rite. It refers to the "other body" that the cunning sorcerer or witch can create with will, to go "out and about" in a ghostly form, or it refers to the immortal twin or other-self beyond the Hedge who is the source of a person's spiritual might and protection. This charm can aid workings to attain to both experiences of these powerful manifestations of self.

47

VII. The Hares *in the* Holes

The charm for making the fruit grow larger and in greater
quantity on the orchard trees, and for making the plants of
the earth come forth in greater quality and abundance is
the same as the charm for making the woman fertile- clay
or dark soil is taken from the land on a Saturday twilight
and mingled with the white of an egg, and the shape of
hare made from it. Then, under a large round moon, next
to a well-charmed blazing fire, the hare statue is bathed in
moonlight and firelight, and the charm is made:

* * *

A *leaping god* when people were free
In th' forests & fields long before me
A hare was he, a hare was she,
Fire & fierce, a hare was he.
Hare weird, *life overflowing*
Fire *burning*, furious *running*,
Darting hare, life overflowing
In th' forests & fields long before me,
A *help* for me if *it may be*.

* * *

The hare statue then must be told what *need* it has been
summoned for, the Hare-Weird should very much pleaded
with, and it should be placed on the mantle of the house- or
in a shelter in a tree overlooking the fields and orchards
out of doors. On the next Friday that follows whatever day
the full moon of your first rite fell, another hare should be
made, the same way, with the same charm said by a fire that
contains wood from the first fire. That hare should be buried

49

on the land somewhere, along with an egg, in a hole that is dug but will be opened again and refilled. The powers of the land must be given milk and honey or wine at the first digging of this hole. On the next Friday that follows, craft another hare, and charm it in the same manner in front of a fire at night made with some sticks from the previous fire, and bury that hare in the same hole with an egg- and so on, the hole becoming full of hares and eggs. Do this for eight Fridays, meaning that the hole will never have more than nine eggs and nine hares.

PURPORT

The initial gathering of earth is the only one that should be done at twilight on Saturday. Any other earth needed can be taken on any day. Also, on the Fridays that the sorcerer charms a new hare by the fire, it doesn't matter what phase the moon is- thought the first day that the first hare is charmed, it should be a full moon. That initial full moon need not be on a Friday, but it would be especially powerful if it were. The first earth gathered on a Saturday can be placed aside, to await the full moon day before the first hare is actually sculpted.

VIII. The Cross *of* Witching

The Cross of Witching, which empowers any rite when
performed before, or increases the knowledge, cunning, and
vital force of the sorcerer or witch who crosses themselves
daily and nightly:

* * *

Let th' dust 'neath my feet take heed
& th' sky that gazes 'pon me see
This deed of *witchery* sprung from my depths
Which are th' *resounding deeps* of all:

Old Hobb, Crossroads Keeper, th' *Left Hand Sign* I make
Your cunning to my spirit, your instruction 'pon my rite.

Dark King of Elfhame, *Black Lord* who leads th' Hunt
I beat th' ground for *you*
Your strength to my bone & *sinew.*

Queen *of* Elfhame, Royal Lady in linen white
Upon a *milk-white horse*
Queen of *Bones* I salute you
Your *blessings* on this work of Art.

Old Earth & Sky, my *limbs* I spread
Make a cross of me!
Good folk *be* blessed.

* * *

PURPORT

The "Left hand sign" is made by placing the fore and middle fingers of the left hand on the forehead, spread apart, and sliding them down to the bridge of the nose, closing them as you go. It inscribes an upside-down triangle on your forehead-door, the sign of descending fire, and the sign of a goat or ram's horns. The "ground is beaten" for the Dark King with the right foot- three times. The salute of the Lady is given with the arms crossed on the chest and the head bowed a little. When Old Earth and Sky are invoked, the arms should be spread out to the sides in a true cross shape, and their luminosity above and below flood the person.

IX. The Equinox Cross

The Equinox Cross creates an equilibrated state within the
soul of the cunning one. Before it may be assayed, each
must look into themselves and summon two emissaries- two
symbols, in the form of a person or an animal, of all that
is good and beautiful and right within them and perhaps
this world, and all that is harrowing and wicked. When the
crossing charm is made, those two must be "seen" with the
other eyes entering the chest and facing one another- the
"adored one" and the "feared one".

* * *

Let th' dust 'neath my feet take heed
& th' sky that gazes 'pon me see
This deed of *witchery* sprung from my depths
Which are th' *resounding deeps* of all:

I will th' light that men all *adore*
& th' shadow that men all *fear*
To gather in my *soul-house* swiftly
& make forthwith an *equinox* within me.
By *wickedness* I shall be troubled not
& by every harm pass'd *by*
That is th' reward of equal measure
Of day & night, *of* earth & sky.

* * *

55

PURPORT

Like the Crossing given before, the Equinox cross aims at a state of balance. Where the other cross offers the power of earth and sky, of active spirit and material to go into balance bolstered by the chief powers of the Unseen world, this crossing takes on a further personal meaning and *harrows the mind* that typically wishes to disallow entry into the self of a tangible symbol of the darkness and wickedness that it prefers to ignore. The internal equinox does not see the destruction of the good or the evil, but their mingling and co-existence within the being; they begin by facing one another, and then meld into an amorphous but vibrant power. The darkness within us cannot be ignored or destroyed; it must be accepted and integrated in a healthy manner. *The darkness must be made conscious.* The sunlight of consciousness will scatter shadows, and break their power to obsess us, though they will not be obliterated; they will transmute. They will then serve us, by giving us gifts of vital force well purified.

X. The Thunder Crosses

On Thursday at dawn or twilight, approach a strong Oak tree with a generous measure of milk, honey, and wine mingled. Pour it around the roots, and begging pardon and help from the Oak Weird, *Great Weird of Thunders and Life*, ask for a selection of thin but sturdy twigs, and gather them swiftly, begging the weird to preserve in them the sturdy force you need. Place them in a white cloth and return home, to bind them together at the center with red thread, making equal-armed crosses. The red thread should be soaked in an infusion of rue and verbena before they are so used. Standing under the sky, most ideally with thunder rumbling in the distance, place the crosses in a triangle of white flour, and holding the triangl'd hand over them, say:

* * *

Old Matron of Earth & *Watchful Ward* of Sky
Th' Thunders Below & Thunders Above
Ne'er roared so dark & so grim
As they will shake & swell *furious* against him
Who passes *near* these cross'd beams intending harm
To *me*, th' gatherer of this wood
Th' *cunning binder* of these red threads
& to th' family whom I love
& *all* whom my heart cherishes.
Let every entity, be he man *or* no,
Hearken to these conjuries:
Words of *holy force* are placed 'pon these beams
In th' name of Old *Earth* & *Sky*
& captured in th' red threads that *bind* them.

59

Th' *vengeance of fire* awaits that wicked one
Who would confront these holy forms of oak:
Thunder *shaking* their evil minds asunder
Crushing *sinew, vein, & organ,* finally th' heart,
Reducing them to mewling terror, confus'd fear;
That be their *Fate* till they repent & depart.

* * *

PURPORT

With a simple change of wording, small versions of these potent charms can and should be made for the vessel or vessels buried in the charm of protection for the meadow, given earlier in this gramarye. These old charms are the most readily available and useful talismans in the entire folkloric corpus of the Old Way. They are ideal for hanging above the doors of homes, being worn, or carried on the person.

XI. The White *Mommet*
Or
The Work of White Blood and Red Stone

On Saturday at dawn, gather clay or dirt from the earth,
while speaking this charm:

Earth from which *flesh* is drawn
Gather'd by my hand in th' gaze of dawn
As day quick'ns life in *sky* & *leaf*
So let this flesh alike be *quick*
At my will & art, soon all revealed
Let that *quick* be *captured* & *sealed.*
This in th' name *of* Earth & Sky
& th' Elfin Dominion *Below.*

* * *

That night, and better it be if the moon is full, boil the
white blood- the white of a goodly amount of eggs- along
with a good measure of water, whisky or wine, and the
sympathetic materials you have gathered from the one
whom the *Mommet* will become a double for: their
hair, nails, a tooth, spittle, blood, urine, or an article of
clothing that has been worn against their skin. Make this
charm over the seething boil:

White blood, water of *Earth* & *Sky,*
Water of Life strong & sharp,
(or "Life blood of th' *verdant artery*" if you are using
wine)
X's own flesh & entity,
Be stirred to *quick* by heat & flame

63

Growl & bubble with impetuous life
& take th' soil as man takes wife.

* * *

Then mingle the clay and dirt with the mixture, after it has cooled to warm. From this mix form the shape of a man or woman, depending on the shape of the one you work for or against. Take a small red stone, which shall be the heart of the mommet, and in a new pot, boil it in white blood, again composed of white blood, a measure of water, whisky or wine, and sympathetic material not used in the first seething. As the heart boils, say:

Heart of X, *red* & *strong*
Let flame & heat engorge you well
& th' *white blood of life* 'rouse you:
You will beat in th' chest of X soon;
Perhaps you will leap there *long*
Or *cease* in your striving & hasten doom.

* * *

When the white blood has cooled to warm, take the heart and embed it in the chest of the Mommet, in the proper place of a human heart. Cover it in well. Now, again, in a fresh pot, set to boil white blood, a larger measure of water, and a handful of Mugwort, dry or fresh. As the steam rises strong, take a broad forked piece of wood and suspend the Mommet over the steam, face down, with an open hole dug in its head where the mouth should be. Say:

X, this is th' *Breath of Life*
64

Th' whisp of soul, th' *Lunar* wraith that you inhale
This is th' moving *breath* of th' *World,*
Th' *wind of bones,* mare of peace & *strife*
So inhale th' *ghost* & rise from earth's dim bed
Cross th' Hedge *between* th' quick & dead

* * *

Turn the Mommet over and very quickly seal the mouth-
hole over. Inscribe on the Mommet's body the full name
of the other it doubles, as well as their mother's name, if
you know it. Do not use a metal instrument to inscribe
this; use a thorn, a bird's talon, or a sharpened stylus
of wood. Now dress the Mommet, detail it to resemble
the one whose double it will be, as best you may, and
incorporate your last un-seethed sympathetic materials, if
you have any. When you are ready, lie it inside a triangle
of white flour under which has been poured the three
trickle roads, lit only by candles. Baptize it with water and
salt mingled and made pure and strong, the water of
purification, into which a lit candle has been thrust and
extinguished. Baptize it in the name of earth and sky,
and name it as the one that it now lives as double. Take
the living double and show it to the four winds, holding
it up to each direction, declaring his or her name thrice
to each wind. Now the Mommet may be used in the
manner of sympathetic working.

PURPORT

The creation of the White Mommet is the most powerful
spell known to me for the birthing of a living psychic copy of
another person. Properly made, the Mommet is absolutely
bound to the Fate of the person it copies. Any manner of
working can be done on it or to it- and those workings will
affect the other as though that other were present. When not
in use, the Mommet should be kept safely lying on oak leaves
or mosses in a wooden box or some vessel of the like. Of
course, if you have no intention of keeping the Mommet safe,
such a fine home is not needed. You may create Mommets
of yourself, for use in healing or binding workings- if there
is another person you desire, making a Mommet of yourself
and the other is powerful; when both are made, lay them face
to face and bind them together at the waist- around the genital
area with green threads that have been soaked in a Venusian
infusion. Keep them together in a box or dark, enclosed
space; always secret.

Healing threads of golden color can be soaked or bathed in
the smoke of solar herbs and wrapped around body parts
that need healing, after first placing them in a white triangle
of flour and, holding the triangl'd hand over them, invoking
them and charming them to the healing task needed, and
sealing them as you seal the power in the purifying water- with
the triple circle and cross. You will have to experiment with
the proper proportions of dirt and clay along with egg-white to
see what makes the most sturdy mix for the Mommet's body,
lest it crumble apart too easily. Some find that mixing in lots
of finely chopped straw helps to bind the earth/clay together,
but a suitable thick, viscous proportion of earth and clay and
the white blood suffices. I also find that wrapping the body

66

and limbs in cloth tightly and tying it on with a thin twine or cord helps to hold it together, if you can't get the proportions correct. Always treat the Mommet gingerly, unless of course you intend wrath to it.

To "undo" a Mommet without harming the person it doubles, undress it and burn any dressing, remove the names from it, disavow all connections to it, if it be a Mommet that doubles you. "Wash off the name" and baptism with plain salt water (unconsecrated), And show the now simple lump of earth to the four winds, introducing it as "a lump of senseless earth" and bury the rest in come apart in the ground naturally, in peace. The use of "White blood"- egg protein- is an especially potent part of this rite; in the boiling, some of it turns to a soft solid, which must be smashed back down to a semi-liquid for the mixing with earth. Skin is likewise composed of such proteins; the sympathetic resonance is very powerful.

XII. Walking the Trod
or
The Nine Doors Under the Hill

At night, and on the floor of a chamber you can lie
in, or outside in a safe clearing, take a walking staff of
hazel and a good-sized, pleasing stone that has sat on
your hearth for several moons, being warmed by your
hands, your home fires, or candles by which you read
over the space of weeks, and place them in a triangle of
white flour which has been drawn over the three trickle
roads. The stone shall fit easily in the triangle; only the
center of the staff needs to be within, the rest of it lying
outside. Have the flour-triangle lit by taper or flame. Put
a larger ring of flour around you, the triangle, and the
two implements. Have a pillow for your head and other
bed-materials if needs be. Perform the two crossings- the
Cross of Witching and the Equinox Cross- and, if you
like, lay Thunder Crosses around the perimeter of flour.
Go to your roots, in sorcerous concentration, and gaze
upon the staff and stone, and say:

Encircl'd *white* & with th' lamp-light of *spirit*
I speak *words of Art* that embody will
My will to th' stars & shadow-draped sky
To th' field & wood & *staring* Moon
Open th' *doorway below* & give me enter
& safe return again.
With hazel-staff & hearth stone
One to go *forth* & one to come *home*
I stride forth into th' *Otherness.*

69

Now lie down holding the staff, clutching to it if need be, close your eyes, and regress further to your "roots." Go so deep that you go into the depth of the world, and allow the image of a burial mound that you have seen or visited, a sacred Faerie-tree, or an old well, a natural pond, lake or spring, or a cave or hole in the ground, to appear before you- you must will it, and will to be "standing in front of it"- in a fetch body, fed and maintained by will. There should be an oaken door over the opening, if there was an opening, and if not, imagine (such as the case of the hill-mound) that a door is now there, one of oak, at the base of the hill or mound, in a lump of ground aside the spring or pond, or in the tree. In the case of a well, the first door is down at the bottom of the well, glimmering through the water. Let your fetch body shrink to a size that can use the door easily, and stride over to it, and open it. In your fetch body, you should have the hazel-staff with you. When that door opens, light pours down the tunnel beyond, illuminating another door very far in the distance. Plunge down the tunnel to that second door, also of oak. Take a moment to feel how far below the ground that first passage took you, then open the second door. Again, light pours down a long passage, and at the end of that one, you can see another oak door. Go down to it, fly down, run down, but always pause to feel how much deeper you have gone. Do this for nine doors- when the ninth door opens, it opens into a deep region of the World below the Earth. What shall be there is only for you to know or see, though the wise never attempt to guess or desire or imagine what it will be like; let the first thing you see when you emerge be what it is, and as you explore, simply let it become whatever it will. Interact
70

with whatever beings you see or meet that take interest in you, and explore otherwise. When it is time to return, call to the Hearth Stone, and imagine it strongly, and fly, quickly, back the way you came, all in an instant if need be, through the nine doors, hearing them slam as you pass through them, and back to your body lying down. Never allow another to discover you in this state, and disturb you awake suddenly.

* * *

71

PURPORT

Volumes could be written regarding the "Faery regression" into Elfhame or the transformation of the mind into the perceptual "other way of seeing" the Unseen. One thing is certain- this experience is never the same for two people. This particular working places your mind in perceptual contact with the shadow of this world, the region that is a border between the physical, outward world, and the deeper regions of the Unseen beyond. In this other state, nearly anything can be visited- or anyone- and their otherworldly aspect encountered. There are several bits of advice that can be offered here for ease and power, and several suggestions for making this working more powerful

It helps to "hoodwink" yourself or tie a black cloth over your eyes when you lie down. Try to be in as quiet a place as possible until you have mastered this. Do not try too hard to visualize anything; seeing with the inner eyes, the fetch-eyes, is really effortless when mastered. Trying too hard at first will impair your power to gain the trance required. This work is best done on a full moon, or around the time of a full moon, and especially around the time of the "Hidden Festivals", Walpurgis, Beltane, Samhain, and the like. The full moon helps facilitate the transition because its abundant light and subtle power makes the *moon-trods* open and powerful, all over the earth and sky.

The most important part of the descent is *feeling* how deep you've gone- if you begin to truly feel that you've gone down a perilous long way, like a miner who has gone layer after layer down a mine (that sinking feeling when you wonder how you'd ever get out of the mine collapsed) you are doing well. Don't try to see anything; don't expect Faery-kingdoms or enchanted forests. Let any landscape or experience arise, including ones that make no sense or are dream-like and bizarre. They too, have a place in the authentic experience.

If sounds from the environment "here" are distracting you, understand that even masters of this Art must deal with the "twoness" of consciousness- some part of you does maintain a connection with the body while "away" in most cases. Only the deepest of Trod-walks really sever nearly all communication from the prone physical body. You must just accept that the echoes from our world that you are hearing are due to your senses in the flesh still operating, and use will to maintain focus on your quest and inner story. If needs be, in the trance, in your inner eyes, focus strongly on the staff you are holding, a ghostly but identical copy of the one your physical body is grasping. Focus on it only until you've "deepened", then resume explorations.

Always be polite and sensible with anyone or anything you encounter, and if something is threatening, simply run or fly away instantly. Using the Feery-feast to make a petition to the Powers below to allow you access to the Underground world and to help you find your Puckril, or your Fetch-beast, is one of the first workings you should set out on, but never hurry it- you want to be experienced enough to have enough clarity to gain an accurate identification of the Fetch-beast. But obtaining a strong clear communion with your "Other self" beyond the hedge should be your first priority, and it appears first as a beast of some sort. Never try to guess what sort it will be; never, never never. Only allow it to appear as it will. It may also appear as a person, but that is more rare, at least at first. To gain this relationship with the Fetch wins for you a tireless
73

and powerful guide to the riches, attainments, and dangers of the Unseen world, and a staunch protector.

Do not attempt to use a natural location as your "entry point" unless you first go there and give the Watch and Ward of the place offerings of cakes, bread, milk, wine, and honey, any or all of those things. Another use for the Cairn of the Convocation of the Meadow is the speed at which it wins favor from the land-powers for you in a place, making it easy for you to use an opening in that land, near the Cairn, for this voyage. All of the charms, workings, and even the sigil on the cover of this book were won from spirits met while using this technique. An in-depth exploration of any aspect of your being or this world is possible with it. Do not journey too long- no more than 30 minutes at a time (you will find that time means little in the Unseen, anyway) and always journey when you are WELL RESTED- if you are tired when you lie down, you will fall asleep and lose the trance.

XIII. A Sealing Conjuration

To be used after any and all of the conjurations and
invocations given in this work- it will increase their power
tenfold if used at the end of each one.

* * *

This is so, as Providence has woven *thus*;
This is so, by th' King of Heaven & Earth;
Puckril Mighty, Your charge is *clear*, bring it to *pass*.

* * *

PURPORT

This sealing can be placed after any of the words of force given in this gramarye, and the only one that seems to not need it, and indeed, seems *encumbered* by it, is the incantation for the Cross of Witching.

Afterword:
The Faery-Faith, Witchcraft, *and* the Metaphysics of Faery-Elfhame

"'Tis merry, 'tis merry in Fairy-land,
When fairy-birds are singing,
When the court doth ride by their monarch's side,
With bit and bridle ringing;

And gaily shines Fairy-land-
But all is glistening show,
Like the idle gleam that December's beam
Can dart on ice and snow.

And fading, like that varied gleam,
Is our inconstant shape,
Who now like knight and lady seem,
And now like dwarf and ape."

-Sir Walter Scott

* * *

Scrying in fire is a very old custom. When a fire starts to die down, a treasury of glowing embers, all bright orange and ebon black, hisses in the pyre. A few golden serpents of flame still leap, and if you stir the fire, you still get a shower of golden sparks, vanishing off into the night. Most people will look into the weird shift of the ember-pile, seeking to see faces or shapes or visions, but few people step back and just look at the fire as a whole. Like with so many other things, the desire to see *something* obscures the sight of what is *there*.

77

Toss another branch of sufficient size onto the glowing fire and you will see the birth of another swarm of sparks. They flare away in flight for a moment, and they are gone forever. The fire itself- its wood, ash, flame, sparks, embers, and heat, is a model of the entire metaphysical structure of the world. Everything is a model of the whole; this is the secret of the scrying art. Pluck a leaf from a tree and look at it- within the leaf is another tree; down the center of the leaf a thick trunk, and radiating out from it, many thin branches, all draped in the green cloak of the leaf. The tree that was parent to the leaf left its signature on each of its children. Within the nut or seed is the entire hidden legacy of a forest.

Walk if you will on an early morning, near a pond, and find a dewdrop hanging from a branch, and really gaze at it. It is a round mirror of fluid, and in the soft light, you will see the world all around you- look until you can see the pond in the droplet. You can even see yourself quite easily. Within each dewdrop or tear swims an entire ocean, should you take your scrying-droplet to the seashore. Take any good-sized stone from the ground and sit with it; gaze at its rough surface, and you will see the shapes of people, animals, clouds, and many other things suddenly emerge, as your mind assembles their shapes from the skin of the stone. A world entire is to be found in every discrete part of the world, just as a man or woman entire is recorded within every hair from their head, or flake of skin, or drop of blood, or line of spittle.

Long has man sought to explain his origins, but the explanation was known long ago to the ancient seer. Cast a branch onto the fire and see the sparks sail up- from a parent flame comes countless lesser fires. The same, yet different; the fire of these mortal bodies- and of any body- is a spark flown from an immortal fire in an unseen world. That is the revelation of the fire; that is the theme of its ancient story. Like the short-lived spark, we mortals flutter but for a moment in darkness, lighting the way in a rush, and then we are swallowed by darkness again, taken back to the depths of our origins. It is said that by the time a man or woman's life is noticed, it is gone forever-but a rainstorm of new sparks continually comes in its stead.

The Ancients knew that this mortal world of things seen was just the half-glow of an immortal light, another world unseen, and that their lives, bound in temporary casings of the earth and cast into the river of time, were the result of immortal lives which were hidden, yet potent enough to affect even this world. And this truth bound not just men, but trees, mountains, stars, beasts, and all else sensible.

And those lordly and immortal flames known to the Ancients under countless names are beings, like us, but not like us- we are sparks from their fires; and we have the same kinship with them which the spark has for the mother fire, though our duration is limited. Without their fire, we never would have been. And yet, does the fire in the nighted clearing intend to shower sparks about? It is in the nature of fires to shoot forth sparks, at a seeming whim, thoughtless perhaps, or just as a consequence of their heated vibrancy.

And thus it is that a deepest mystery sought by man is answered again by the cackle of a simple fire; it is simply in the nature of the Immortals that gave us our temporary being to send forth sparks of life. Many of the Ancients of the great Southern inner sea believed that the origin of all origins was a thing of perfection, a mystery- but "perfection", to these wise men and women had a few qualifiers on its nature. It was in the nature of perfection to overflow and emanate, just as it was in the nature of perfected beings, such as the mortal sages of legend or Gods, to overflow their wisdom and share it with mankind. With a belief in a "perfect" supreme reality, Plotinus and his fellows were content to view the creation and arising of the world- and all worlds- as a *natural consequence of perfection* on the deepest (or highest) levels.

Are the Immortal Fires of the Unseen World "perfect"? The question is worded too simply; it is clumsy. Perfection is a mesmerizing game in the minds of confused people. The Immortals simply are what they are, and the quest for an answer further is forlorn. However, being what they are, other things come to be as they are.

Strange and sentient forces like the Immortals govern everything, in their own ways. Some in the past have thought it foolish to imagine human-like beings attending to every matter of the human world in some invisible form, being overly concerned about events and goings on here. Fortunately for those who understand the reality of the Unseen, the Immortal Fires need not engage in such pedestrian antics to be the rulers, influencers, and governors of events from the Unseen. Through their very nature and activities, things come to pass here, in the world that is seen, as they must.

Do the governors even know the full reach of their spontaneous influence? I think the answer must be yes, but these rulers never set out to rule. Their influence over mortal events is an unplanned, natural consequence of their existence, though they are certainly aware enough, intellectual and wise enough, to understand the impact and reach of their presences and to understand how their position in the Fateful unfolding of things allotted them this position of power.

It is the finest sort of power, really: the sort that is taken without taking; an effort made without effort. It is the spirit of any river that will teach you this lesson, if you want it- the river makes no effort to flow; it simply lets flow occur and moves along. The river did not plan for the ground to be sloping, nor did it plan to break the ground at a spring; It did not plan to flow, and yet, the water finds itself in a position where the ground slopes, and it effortlessly goes along. Without doing anything, it flows and crashes and falls and flows again, and over time, even the hardest stone must yield to it. The great Earth itself opens for the river, carving out kingly valleys. The river has penetrated stone and shaped the land, but never once did it *try* to.

Steal the water from the river and place it in a round cup; watch how the water becomes round, spontaneously, easily, smoothly. Pour that same water into a square chest and watch it become square. It conforms to whatever is there with powerful gentleness yet unstoppable power. Throw that water on a hillside; watch how it finds the bottom of the hill with perfect speed and grace, never once taking a wrong turn, following the shortest and easiest path, simply conforming to the realities of gravity and surface and atmosphere. The power of water is very wise, and yet again, it didn't choose to be. It simply let be.

* * *

These Lordly Ones in the non-spatial, perpetual world, they were called The Gentry, the Good Neighbors, the Good Folk, the Sidhe, the Hill-Folk, the Hidden People, the Huldu-folk, the Elfin people, the Hidden Company, Faerie, and a hundred other names in various countries. These names all imply one thing- that the Lordly Ones, our immortal sources and rulers,

81

our perpetual kin and neighbors, are hidden, concealed, and worthy of great respect. Even the term "faerie" records it; it is a corrupted descendant of "Fatae", the Fateful power that shapes things.

Among their infinite number unseen is found the key to understanding the Gods of the Heathen world. These living powers can be encountered as ageless, powerful, angry, peaceful, ugly, beautiful, wise, foolish, kindly, and dangerous. These are the "spirits" known by any culture, anywhere in the world. The Faery-Faith is the final reflection, in modern times, of the ancient animism of our own ancestors. It is our ancient testament of wisdom, covered in the drapery of centuries of evolving lore and influences. And the Elfin inhabitants of the Unseen are the powers that stand behind our destiny, and perhaps the destiny of all, if one accords them their proper place, under another cultural guise, in the unfolding of human spiritual insight.

For the Fae-world is the fire, and our world the pale luminescent halo of the fire. When a man rages at the world around him, his anger is a spark, a tiny spark and shadow, of what rage truly is. The Fae-world contains the pureness of things, the reality of things, the perpetual pure fountain that is matrix to things, and everything that spontaneously leaps from the unseen into the seen is only a passing simulacrum, a ghost, a fraction of its source. Whatever is thought ugly here is only a hint of the unutterable depths of ugliness and darkness that exist.

A woman may be thought beautiful in our world, but the Ladies of the Faery World are true beauty incarnate. A mortal woman's beauty hides some flaw; it is said that there is no perfect apple; but the apples of Elfland are flawless, insofar as a mortal understands the term "flaw". Where an apple in this world offers temporary nourishment to the earth of the body, the apples of the unseen world offer the lasting sweetness of immortality.

Thus it is that the apple was accorded the position in ancient lore of the food of the dead, and the food of the deathless Gods alike. For the dead have seen the grave's own revelation; they have seen and felt the walls between what is mortal and what is immortal fall apart and fade away. In the tomb or barrow, the veil dividing the warm haze of mortality and the fire of the immortal is gone. The dead cease to "be" the entangled identities they picked and plucked and assembled from years in the world that is seen, and become something deathless. The mortal fire is gone; the immortal fire remains.

For the truth is this: the spark that is the undying, secret *materia* of each man or woman emerged from an immortal flame in an unseen world, and there, it is an immortal spark. But by virtue of its presence and existence in the unseen, a corresponding movement in this world had to occur; the movement "here" is the birth of a life. What moves there, affects here, and vice-versa. There is reciprocity between the worlds, a deep dependence of types.

The warm mortal life involves a mortal fire which resonates most near to the twin immortal fire, and those two fires conjoined (held together by a fine weave of light that binds them in some mysterious manner across the border between time and the timeless) are the source of the mind and will, the very essence of your own naked awareness and ability to be conscious, to know anything at all.

A body of mortal earth, twin to an immortal earth, is receiver of your mind, home and barrow, hall and cloak. It receives the mortal fire as readily as the ground beneath your feet drinks in deep veins of magma and lets them swirl and flow in its darkest depths. Everywhere are the elements mingled, without fault or difficulty.

A mortal water flows in you, corresponding to an immortal water unseen, and from that mortal water, that lunar, aquatic entity, arises a ghostly etheric double of the body, the "ghost" or "wind of the bones", and within it is the subtle elemental substratum which allows for the functioning of the senses and nerves, the home of feelings and sensations and emotions, as they pour in from the fires above, or from the senses about. This water is the receiver of genetic legacy and blood, passed from parent to offspring in this world.

Within you, the contact of the mortal fire with the mortal water of your being creates a boil, a seething, and finally a mist- and that mist, that "mortal air"- the "wind of the flesh"- is the provider of motion and energy to the earth and water of the corpse. At death, that wind rushes or seeps out- the breath of life itself gone back to the home of winds.

The ghost of the body, at death, moves in the subtle, dreamlike world of the moon-realm, very much within the mortal world but unseen- on the misty borders of this world. That ghost, that wraith, cannot persist forever; soon it returns to the primal waters that were its origin, dissolving in cessation after a short or, more rarely, a long period of perceptual time- a time spent on the "Ghost Roads". What part of itself it passed on to offspring during its time connected to a body of earth, by mingling its water and blood with the water and blood of another, those parts persist in the life of those offspring and

84

the generations that arise later.

* * *

The mortal fire, dragged along in the watery body of the ghost, undergoes many adventures and journeys on the "ghost roads". This is the phantasmagoric time of transition through the subtle world in which the darkest dreams and fears and brightest fantasies of the deceased arise as phantasms and characters to accost them, to enthrall, teach, and torment them. The "dark wet hound" the dreaded *Dobarcu* or the Black Dog- a "water dog" that may appear in many forms- is the chief challenger on this road. The guilt or fears of the deceased are embodied within it, and it is the hindrance that comes between the wandering ghost and its goal of reaching "home".

"Home" may be thought of as peace, rest, illumination, or truth; but for the being in this long transition, it may be envisioned as anything. The ghost-road is nothing less than the *process of resolution back to the depths* that are our origins. The grave-mound or burial place is the passageway into the earth and the underworld, and as folklore and the Old Ways have long stated, it is the Land itself that is the outer shell of the Unseen world; we reach the unseen and unknown *through* the Land, through the merging of powers with tree-roots and hills and springs and wells. The Ancestors who have made the transition into the "next world" meet us still through the ground, through the stones and trees. They are here, still, in a very real fashion.

The World of Faery is perceptually below the earth; For too long we have looked only upward to the sky for our vision of the Otherworld. The Ancients looked down to see the sacred

85

dimension of the ground and forests and rivers. They also looked up; the stars are doors to unseen worlds, too- even Faery- but the first human religions were things of the ground, and that wisdom has become crucial to us again, today, living in a world where we are alienated from things fleshy and earthy, and unable to see the natural world in terms of sacredness.

Many barriers and tests appear on the Ghostly trail that leads below the earth, west, or beyond; vast ravines that cannot be crossed, great raging rivers with only a precarious bridge no thicker than a blade's edge; impenetrable walls of thorns, raging fires that consume half of the world; flocks of demonic birds that mock and screech at the traveler, rains of bile of phlegm, rivers or oceans of blood, and the like. There is a key, known to the ancients of the oldest wisdoms, to passing through all of these challenges, and that key is found in one sentence, best committed to memory now: **"Go straight through without fear or hesitation."**

For these barriers cannot harm the subtle body, and they cannot hinder or hold back a being who plunges straight through them, going forward without hesitation. They are only impassible to those who pause, hesitate, seek a way around, and cannot summon the courage to just go straight through. They are illusions; to those wrapped in unwisdom, Faery is a world of illusions, of inconstant shapes. But then, the same may be said about the world of mortal men.

When beings such as the perilous birds screech and mock, the proper response is to "simply listen"- listen without care or concern for their mockery, nor with eagerness to be rid of the mockery- and then to move on. When the rains of terrible fluids adhere to one's ghost-body, one must take a care not to brush it off; one must simply move on, calmly detached.

86

To attempt to cleanse oneself through a flurry of activity will cause one to become confused and lost.

To be "lost" on the ghost roads is a mental trap, a trap of fear or hesitation, and some may remain lost for ages. The Black Dog likewise cannot hold back those who walk right by it without fear. This may be easier said than done, for the ghost-roads harrowing cannot be passed with ease if a person, in their earthy life, was long conditioned to hesitate, give in to fears or guilt, or lack bravery.

The visions of the ghost-roads are projections of mental states; they are resolutions of the strengths and flaws of the released and journeying mind. The Black Dog is the very manifestation of the forces of life itself, justice incarnate for those who seek freedom and truth, but who have acted and thought in such ways as to transgress against virtue and rightness.

Those blessed with the favor of the Faery realm, and those wise in other ways, wise enough to have established a living connection with beings of the otherworld during life, may have guidance down these roads. There is a *guardian entity* that follows each through his or her life; though few gain conscious contact with it during a life of earth.

Appearing in the form of some beast, or of a contrasexual being of great beauty or grace and power, This Fetch or Guardian is a great mystery of the ancient way. Some say that it is a separate being entirely, a spark of fire that flew from the same source as the person, and thus a kin being, protecting and helping its kin through the strange initiatory transformations of this life, and guiding that person beyond to truth or peace.

Some say it is an aspect of the deepest or highest wisdom of the person- for the immortal and timeless realm, when judged in relation to this world, allows for such paradoxes to exist and to be resolved. Can the immortal fire be completely absorbed into the mortal life, seemingly forgetful, informing the mortal personality which is arisen without full recall of its higher nature, and yet, that same immortal fire still be actively working on another level to reach "itself" deep in the human world?

These are truly recondite matters that defy easy explanation, and indeed, need not be explained away. When one introduces the idea of the *timeless* into the equation, and the great mystery of the otherworld, it must be remembered that something can be "myself and not myself" *at the same time*. Whatever the case, one thing is for certain: whatever it may be, the guardian exists, it is a link between mortals and the immortal world, it is an unfailing source of protection and wisdom, and is a great boon to those who can find conversation and experience of it, and maintain this link. Great wickedness in life will drive it away, perhaps forever.

A final point comes when the wandering ghost is resolved from the ghost roads and the predations of the Black Dog, and lo and behold- there is the dissolution of that ghostly double. Without the grounding support of earthy body or watery wraith, the mortal fire is released to be overwhelmed and absorbed by the light of the undying fire that is its transpersonal twin. This may seem catastrophic- like a second death, in fact; but it is not; it is a great "remembering", a great resolution and return to the deathless state, the awakening of the Faery-nature.

To the extent that a person truly identified themselves with the mortal elements, ignorant of the deeper roots of self, that person's self-concept and personality must of necessity be lost in this metamorphosis; to the extent that wisdom guided a person to be aware of the *temporary* and *selfless* nature of these arrangements of mortal elements that we identify so easily with, and to make a vast and clear channel of their minds, an "open and hollow bone" for the undying light to shine through, that person will be spared any pain during this event.

The wise will notice that this discussion of a process of effort, testing, purgation, and illumination after death has a perfect parallel to what the path to wisdom is like *in life*, as well- for they are truly the same process. To undergo this process during life, and reach the final illumination constitutes "dying before you die"- true initiation.

* * *

Each being in this world, human or animal, and perhaps others, are Sidhe or Faery-beings ourselves, awaiting a transition back to the Fae-state, and many of the Hidden Ones of the unseen are awaiting a transition back to the human state. It does not do to think of Human and Sidhe as two separate things, but as two sides of a single being, a being with two natures. There, in the Fae-world, the Immortal Fires that are our true origins declare our destinies and Fates. When the conditions are met, when the "outward" cycles of the world meet in harmony with the strange inward conditions of Faery, we journey in "reverse" to this world again. Every new life eventually meets its destiny, and then dies. These matters are hard to measure; destiny can be obscure or even invisible to us who observe another's life.

89

This body of mortal earth, which men and women so often solely identify with, is a body of *goblin earth*- it is unseelie earth, titanic earth, an earth that devours. The earth, as all elements, has two poles of expression; the mortal earth is both a fruitful power- its noble nature, its *seelie* or luminous nature-and a devouring power- its goblin nature. It gives, but when its polarity changes, it consumes and takes as well. The waters are themselves beguiling, or thirst-curing; the fires are greedy and consuming or warming and healing; the airs are fickle and inconstant or the bearers of the breath of inspiration.

To be alive in a body of earth, is to slowly watch one's own body devour itself, as King Kronos, the ancient Greek Earth-titan, devoured his own children. The goblin nature of the elements is one that tends towards disarray and destruction, and in the mortal world, one must forever behold the endless shifting of polarities. What is perpetual and whole in the Fae-world is a shifting light-show here, a constant ebb and flow.

The mighty seasons themselves- the greatest expressions of power- show the great cycle to which our every mortal fiber is attuned. "The ebb and the flow" reveals something of the nature of power as we know it- it is dynamic, it is a process. But what underlies the dynamism and process? The language here is dangerous; it may suggest that some-*thing* under-lies or "lies beneath it", some tangible *thing* that is eternal and unchanging. But that *thing*, whatever it may be, is no-*thing* in the sense that humans tend to know things. Thus, it is perfectly truthful, if tricky and subtle, to declare "*nothing* underlies the shifting of power".

The shifting of power is everywhere; it is everything; it has no "underneath". In this world,. a stone may lie on the ground below a tree-branch, a real "thing lying below something else",
90

but the mystery of Elfhame's immortal essence is not a *thing* like a stone, nor can the cycles that bind all have an "outside" or "underneath". But our use of language forces us to the simple level of stones and branches, of tangible things, of spatiality, and of duration. When attempting to describe the mysteries of the Unseen world, this language is severely limited. We must think on a more subtle level and be prepared to move into trans-rational spaces of mind.

"What is perpetual and whole" in the Faery world, or "of" the Faery world, is a strange and eldritch *condition or a quality*, not a *thing*. Process must be universal; it must have effect even the Immortal world; what makes that place *immortal*- and the great beings of that world immortal- is a *condition* that is not *disrupted by change*. For entities or beings, that is a condition of *mind*; for whatever else must exist somehow- the immortal twins of the mortal elements, for instance, that is a purified vision of their true nature, had by the immortal beings themselves.

In light of this "strange and eldritch condition" by which the Elfhame-immortals *persist as truly immortal,* we can still, with truthful and somewhat poetic hearts, announce that Faery, unlike the mortal world, is "whole, eternal, and immortal" or "beyond the perceptual cycles that entrance mortal men", even if the omnipresent force of cycling and power-process still exists in some manner "there", as it must.

One perspective further adds to this: the entire edifice of the folkloric tradition records that "time" in Faery is meaningless or warped- mortals spending a day there have found that years have passed in the mortal world. Perception of cycles, and *how cycling processes affect living power* and *mind* are experienced as different between these two worlds. This is what happens

91

when one moves from a world perceived in terms of *quantity* to one which is an expression of *quality-* and this, more than any other use of language, sums up the relationship between the Faery-world and the Mortal world.

* * *

The immortal spark of fire that is the twin of the mortal fire of the mind, the truest mind, as it were, only observes these shiftings, ebbs and flows of the mortal world by virtue of its connection to that mortal, perceiving fire which must be encased in earth, drenched by water, and blown by airs. The undying spark's very presence brings true *life* to the elemental system, acting as a perfect partner to it, sharing in its experiences, but is not ultimately subject to it; it is not harmed by anything that occurs to the mortal elements, nor do the births or deaths that it shares harm it. This undying spark is a thing "outside of space and time" as we know them.

When we feel a person's heart is still, we say that they are dead, but *stillness is not itself death.* When we see a person moving and walking down the street, we say that they are alive, but *motion is not itself life.* What makes us "living" or "dead" is not stillness or motion alone, but the presence of the undying fire and its mortal fire twin, that which gives us the power to dream and conceive, to remember and grasp abstraction, to assemble reality at every moment with imagination, and add *will to our motion,* creating the Art that is life.

That spark of undying fire within you, or perhaps "of" you, (for it is not spatially bound) is your Faery-nature, your fateful nature, your undying nature. It is the perpetual offspring of a mightier source-flame in the unseen world. That source- the Mother of your true clan, the *Matrona* or Faery-Grandmother who sits and watches over you and all of those truly kin to you on the spiritual level (and many other levels)- was herself born of the most immense source of all: the darkest matrix of origins, which is itself vast beyond reckoning, but which appears clothed in cobweb and shadow, in abstraction and metaphor, in folklore and myth, as a great queen, hidden and potent, terrible and wise, weaving Fate. And that Great Queen has a husband, a mighty Hunter and balancer of the scales of life and power, protector of Nature, a consort of awesome might who is Father to all, in his way.

People in the past foolishly turned against the wisdom of Fate, and against the awesome spirit of life-power in nature, that true Father, excoriating him as "The Devil". But he is closer to the mainstream conception of "God" than any "devil"- the fatherly power of life, wind, fertility, rain, thunder, and even wrath at times. The being in traditional folklore that resonates more with the "chief fallen angel" figure is the Lord of Light, called Puck or *Robin Goodfellow* by some, and by countless other names- goatish, satyrish, cunning and gregarious, he is the mediator between heaven and earth, the intellectual spirit of cunning who, with the aid of his fiery ministers, taught mankind the secrets of culture and technology, the very first sorceries.

He is "son" of the Fateful mother and the mighty Huntsman-Father, in the same manner that we are all sons and daughters of this primordial pairing. He is a prince of Faery-Elfhame, and the arch-enchanter, tutelary spirit, and chief initiator of many a Witch-man or woman and coven from history. He remains in that role to this day, able to be contacted by the wise. No invocation to "Earth and Sky" should end there; to "Earth, Sky, and the Mediator between Them" is the proper form, if one wants power- the true ancient trinity.

It is amazing to see the powers of age, unwisdom, and unbelief bring their terrible "dwindling" force on the deep Lords and Ladies; those who were once Gods appear to have shrunk into the diminutive folk of legendry and folklore; and yet, even in miniature, these icons are only fateful masks for great powers who are agelessly potent. The Fayerie-People are not simply forgotten relics of a bygone age, or just fancies; they are immortal forces of great might, danger, and beauty. It is the treasure of our Western folklore that it preserves so much, even in a greatly diminished, sanitized manner; the very essence of the true Ancestral Tradition of Europe, and all of Old Europe's gemlike wisdom, is found in the pages of fairy stories.

The Faery-Faith is concerned with all aspects of the natural world and mankind- not just the Great Powers, but those many other powers that arise from their interactions and their eternal unseen magistry and sovereignty. The Immortal Fires that are the sources of human families and beasts and other living beings, the Immortal Fires that are offspring of the First Queen and King, are no less important to the broad view of the old Faith. Ruling as Queen and Kings under each land and in each forest, one may never know what Gentry or Court is near at hand when they set out to explore the landscape.

One thing is for certain, however- all places are drenched with life and orders of life, seen and unseen, and within the unseen, those orders of life sometimes form a hierarchy. This is not so strange; even in the forest, certain predators form the apex of a chain of feasting and living- a power that they didn't take with thought and calculation, but through the natural way of things.

94

Human political and social power is often taken by force; the power among beasts, and among the powers unseen, is a function of the water-course flow of the unfolding of power. Humans are beings of a special intellect; there is no doubt that it is the use and misuse of this power that leads to corruption and scandal among human beings, but the powers unseen are also possessed of that awakened intellect, and intrigue can exist among some of them. But the land is not divided up so easily; theriomorphic beings, strange elemental beings, and countless other shapes and images and beings exist even in the smallest of stones or wells or caves or streams.

One cannot begin to catalogue them all; Faery-Elfland is a non-spatial and timeless dimension occupied by a range of forces and beings, just as this world is; though this world is experienced as spatial. Though many ranges of intellect and consciousness exist, nearly all can influence both the seen and unseen world in various ways, making the skill of trance and extraordinary sight an important skill for the wise to learn. To gain the power to interact with the unseen is crucial for deeper well-being and wisdom.

When we approach the faery-faith as a lens with which to examine our own origins, we discover, as I said before, our origin in the Faery-world or the unseen. In this world we are partly beings of this elemental earth, and partly the wayward children of Faery Ladies and Lords who live unseen and perpetual.

The old worship of the "Mothers" brings us to the doorstep of this idea; over each of our vast human families watch the First Mothers, the Immortal Fires from which many sparks flew and found purchase in the unseen as Faery-offspring, and who, in the rotations and strange conditions of the seen and unseen world, came to experience life in this world, rotating back and forth between the human and the faery. No mistake or "sin" or accident drove this rotation, this procession of mystery; it is merely the nature of the unfolding of things.

We are all kin; it is said that to the living, we owe respect, and to the dead, we owe the truth. When we approach our deepest mothers, when we are finally resolved after our journey back to Faery, it is those who gave truth to the dead, to the unseen world, and to those around them in life who will win the *secret metamorphosis* which forever establishes them as immortal fires in the unseen world. The rotation back and forth between seen and unseen is not a truly eternal process, but one that has an "endpoint", in a manner of speaking, for a perceptually individual being.

What flies out from the Mother-Fires as an eternal spark is perhaps only the raw material of what a true eternal fire can be; perhaps it must be tested and tempered in the shifting and alternating vision of mortality before winning to that true highest awareness, and being endowed with the vestments and implements of the perpetual life beyond forgetfulness and change. The Mothers of each of us impose a strict rule, but also a love; the most wicked of us can be banished from their presence or given the strictures of a hard Fate in some other way to repay the debts they owe to them or to other kin.

The Mothers, themselves embodying the great synergy of forces that becomes a *Great Fateful Power* that guides all things towards an unknown destiny, lay down the ancient laws of Faery- that we must strive to be hospitable, generous, respectful of the sanctity of private and secret things, neat and simple in our living, loving order and beauty, and strive to avoid being rude, selfish, cruel, and gloomy of heart.

96

The Mothers are not capricious; they move in circles of a greater wisdom, a deeper wisdom and vision which they impart to all of their deserving offspring. They appear pale and ghastly to weep, at times, before the death of a family member; they preside over mortal births of their children to allot blessings and restrictions.

The idea of a "testing till perfection" for all of us is, of course, speculative. It may be that the "two poles" of the being (the faery and the human) are simply natural halves of a whole, that life and death occur as natural aspects of their interplay, and that the secret metamorphosis is a fine-tuned harmony that arises *between* them naturally and eventually- and no further explanation is needed. But beings other than ourselves observe the processes involved; they guide, protect, reward, punish, and remain involved. To what end, none but those most wisely attained may finally say.

It is true that the operations of the Faery-metaphysics can create knowledge of the unseen; they can create visions and a bridge between the mortal and immortal aspects of a being, awakening the "two sights" that all Faery-seers since time immemorial have been known to possess. The two worlds can be collapsed into one, in the mind and body of a cunning human being or true Witch. But even before the arising of special gifts won through occult effort or given as mystical gifts at birth, the heart of each person has a strong thread of Fate woven into it, tugging and urging each towards a destiny that is unavoidable.

"Letting go" and letting the power flow through you, not becoming either dominated by or ignorant of one's desires and urges towards various persons, places, and things, and

97

thus avoiding unhealthy entanglements with binding powers, is an ancient art of guidance that can bring much peace and progress to a person's life. This is the "hollow bone" mystery that protects the wise on their way.

The true Faery Faith and the Metaphysics of the Witchcraft of Elfhame teaches and offers the following attainments:

1. Knowledge of the Immortal Beings that stand behind our worlds and families

2. The way of living rightly and with peace in this world of sentience and of sacred, binding natural processes

3. The certainty of a destiny that will be fulfilled, and a life beyond this one

4. A means of gaining uncommon and extraordinary wisdom and skills that are born from contact with the unseen world-true sorcery and the Art.

5. A path of respect and truth which can assure peace and ease on the journey after this life is over

6. The blessings of beings in the unseen world, their aid during this life in the form of fertility, plenty, peace, and protection.

It is my hope that this tome of Lore and Art will help guide you on the way to any and all of these great goals, attainments, and ends.

For the wise, or those whose hearing is endowed with fire, a rainstorm can teach a magic song. A rumble of thunder, a soft white sky, and a deep cool announces the spell's beginning. In obscure paleness and mist above, royal drops form and fall. The earth below is moistened- green becomes greener- and to the feeling man's secret senses, a thousand unseen hands in the ground rejoice at the water. Like a great and ancient king and his bride, there is a lasting embrace; the world is put to right. With fierceness or softness, life passes between the great Lord and his Queen. It is the oldest song. The storm only appears as arching fire and falling water; it is an undying theme that wears a mask. The living soul celebrates; the spirit knows its heritage. The royalty of Elfhome spread their tents and trot their horses across fields made fertile by rain.

Appendix:
A Letter to Mr. Wavren, *Concerning* How One May Enter into
The Experiential Dimension of the True Old Ways
And the Path of True Witchery *or* Sorcery

* * *

Dear Mr. Wavren:

Blessings of the Summer Stars and the *Hidden People in the Land* on you and yours.

I received your letter and read it with great interest. I am pleased to make the acquaintance of a gentleman such as you who clearly shares a love for a spiritual aesthetic that I adore so, and a strain of wisdom- a stream of wisdom- that is definitive to me. We are few and far between, friend; modern occultism and witchcraft is a circus of harmful, lame, or pointless influences, which do nothing but lead people away from precisely where they all wish to go anyway: to the wholeness and unique wisdom which is cryptically yet organically embedded in the land beneath their feet.

What makes the case of you, Mr. Wavren, of such particular interest to me is the fact that you have a grasp of the deeper meaning of "aesthetic" already- and you are a scholar, making his way through academia's wilderness. We will need people in the future who can speak the language of academia, to justify to the clique-ish throng of the over-intellectual, self-declared elite our existence on paper. Naturally I don't feel that we need to be "justified", but I must say, it always helps to grant a certain respectability in the outside world if one of us can read and write well!

Aesthetic is all important; more important than dogmas or doctrines. The language of the deep mind, and therefore of the deep world, is not words, but images and feelings. The Land itself is the supreme embodiment of the ultimate spiritual aesthetic- and you already know of what I speak, I think; Witchcraft is, of course, sorcery; it is a willed, specific practice with specific themes, ideas, ideals, forms, and metaphysics; but Witchcraft is part of something larger that extends beyond the triangle and circle, beyond the forest clearing, and beyond directed sorcerous will- it is part of a *relationship* between people and everything else.

And when I say "everything else", I mean "The Land"- because "The Land" does not just refer to the dirt and soil and grasses and trees; much like the occult concept of "The World", it refers to the totality of things seen, and, within the Land, on the other side of the Hedge, or through the grave-doors that penetrate the land, we have all that is unseen. Together, *seen* and *unseen* are symbolized by "The Land".

Relationship is a very, very important concept to the true Old Ways, though most will not see it. The first Witches- the first True Sorcerers- channeled the Art through relationship. The formation of relationships is the key to gaining power- memorize that, Mr. Wavren; it may help you immensely in the future, in all you do. Humans have always been in awe of the power of relationship, and used it- from rich families creating relationships with other powerful families to make their own power greater, to people with problems forming relationships with counselors to gain the needed power of healing- relationship is the river-valley through which power flows.

Humans today are a sad lot; we've forgotten something essential about the truth regarding ourselves and the Land; we believe that we must *form* a relationship with the Land, because we reduce the land to another "agency" or "thing" outside of us, but the Land cannot be so reduced; it can be perceived that way, yes, but perception has a dangerous underside. For everything that is seen, nine things are unseen- perception in the usual sense of the word is dangerous not for what it contains, but for what it conceals. When we do not perceive the whole picture, we are in danger of behaving or thinking inappropriately.

We do not have to *form* a relationship with the Land; we already *have* a relationship with it; one that cannot be stripped from us. When a person re-actualizes the primal knowledge of that relationship, the greatest channel of power that can exist re-opens. The Land's voice is then heard; and, since the Unseen powers are part of the Land, experienced perceptually through the Land, their voices are also heard. The dead- all of the dead of this world, are merged in the ground; it is a great convocation of powers. The First Sorcerers heard them with great clarity, and they learned from them how to experience this world in radically different ways than just the simple manner in which Nature has seen fit to endow us all.

When one lives on the Land as a *part* of it, one has a very different experience of it than most people. In my mind's eye, as in my outer life, I have dwelled in small wooden cottages, amid green forests and fields that radiated both the peace of the rural, but the scents of the untamed and clean. When a person does that, it cleanses them. It begins to restore some "sanity"- for the word "sane" derives, after all, from the Latin "sanus" meaning "whole" or "healthy". To be "whole" is to be "sane"- and to be "whole" is possible only when you destroy the hateful and persistent sense of isolation we all feel.

Then, on those same fields and in those same forests, I see and have seen creatures- rabbits, hares, snakes, owls, timber rattlers, wrens, possums, dogs, deer, hawks... each of them another part of the Land, another force of the whole, like me. When you are sane, you can hear them speak, too.

Friend, never let academia or study seduce you so much that the "other voice" and the "other perception" in you is forgotten. When you gaze upon a tree outside, or an animal, or even a vivid painting, you see much; your senses give you a feast of information drawn seemingly from the outside of you- but don't stop there. If you pay attention, and "separate the subtle from the coarse", you will see how every experience of sense also has a twin "subtle" impression. It is an impression, a feeling, and you will find that it is a different impression or feeling if you happen to be looking at a person, as opposed to a tree or a cat.

That impression cannot be "tracked" back to something that is coming "into you" from a sense-portal. It seemingly arises from within, though at the same time as the sensory experience. That, friend, is the beginning of your search for experiential power. It is not easy for most to disabuse themselves of the vibrant flood of sensory coarseness and the intellectual modeling that occurs so rapidly and spontaneously on top of it, to deal in any satisfying way with these subtle impressions, but you can do it with some effort.

But never too much effort, Mr. Wavren. Too much effort creates the "energy of resistance"- which in turn empowers the coarse states that block our subtle senses. The perfect golden mean must be found between too much effort, and not enough. Through this understanding, if you can manage to unpack it, you will find the key to many subtle attainments.

* * *

Friend, the Hedge exists, and it never dies; it is the point "between" too much effort and too little- the frequency of awareness that allows for liberation from one-sided fixation on the coarse consciousness and senses. There is a powerful, Unseen world out there, Mr. Wavren, containing within it intelligences and beings like us (some of them) and then many who are nothing at all "like" us. But to each of them, whether or not we know it, we have a hidden relationship. That hidden relationship- which is, of course, the same one you have to the Land- is the very reason that a conscious relationship can be built; if some essential and lasting connection wasn't there between you and everything else, then no sort of "other" connection could come into existence. Nothing is created from nothing.

Naturally, you will not want a conscious relationship with every power; some are to be shunned for their destructiveness, dumbness, alien-ness, or danger otherwise. But you will discover, to your great and secret joy, that when you penetrate the hedge fully for the first time, certain other beings "over there" already have a conscious relationship with You. None of us are alone. The Fetch-beings that guard and maintain certain hidden relationships with us are real, just as real as you or I, and they wait for us to become conscious of them- so that, in that two-way conscious relationship, power can flow. They can help us; we can help them.

My work, like the work of any writer, evolves. My first book (The Witching Way) I think was good- appropriate to its time, and it presents (again, in my opinion) many important models for understanding some key concepts of the Art. However, I have refined my understanding in countless ways since then. My most recent volume, "The Resurrection of the Meadow" is a reflection of that, with "The Horn of Evenwood" being somewhere between. All of the material given in these books is potent "seed material" for those, like yourself, who have the in-born love for the true sorcerous Aesthetic. It can cause some interesting shoots and blossoms to emerge.

But I'm not in this for calcified knowledge. The supremely powerful sorcerer is a supremely flexible being- a *shape changer*. Seeds go into the ground. They break; they change; they grow into new shapes. That's the way of things, the way of power.

Every paper you write for the Academics will become like a dead thing, even if it is full of powerful information. Academics, in my experience, want everything to be written down in one place, easy to access, and reliable. They tend towards a certain inertia. And then, at the same time, the most discerning among them realize that they can't ever reach the theoretical "final perspective"- the state of knowledge is always changing, and they realize that their lives are an endless paper chase, which most then try to justify as "the natural way of science" or the "nature of knowledge", or "the nature of things".

They're not wrong. But it appears to me that they're grasping at the natural reality of evolutionary change and declaring it as though they were the first to realize it. It is as though they're embarrassed a bit that their forefather academics tried so

106

fear here; most people today, the isolated masses, are already technically *in-sane*, not whole.

No, madness in a sense that transcends the usual meaning of "insane" is the danger- spiritual predation and the consumption of your life force. I don't think you need to worry about that, friend; if you find yourself getting too jittery, too dis-arranged, unable to sleep, eat, or delusional, simply take a break for a while, a good "red rest" in the blood and bones of this world.

But a time is coming when you will have a life on the Other Side of the Hedge, and there, a powerful non-human person will Harrow you. They will pick you apart and purify you of things, tear dear things away from you, because these powers know what holds you back from your goal of Wholeness. You may not thank them at first, but you will later. It is my sincere belief that you will not attain that experience until you are prepared to handle it, so worry not.

* * *

I sincerely hope that some of the things I have said to you here help you in your beginning quest. Let me tell you where the quest ends: in a small house or cottage, somewhere in a green place, distant from the hustle and bustle of madness, far from those places where herds of humans drown in their own redness and industry. It ends with you living *with* the Land, dwelling with the Living *and* the Dead, knowing the sacred powers, feeling the serenity of sanity. There is no greater attainment, Mr. Wavren, than *lasting peace*.

May the King and Queen of the Pale People Below welcome you warmly!

R.A.